PIRATES AROUND THE WORLD

Terror on the High Seas

# Sir Henry Morgan

on Nardo

Mitchell Lane
PUBLISHERS
P.O. Box 196
Hockessin, DE 19707
www.mitchelllane.com

**Mitchell Lane**
PUBLISHERS

Printing      1      2      3      4      5      6      7      8

Anne Bonny
Black Bart (Bartholomew Roberts)
Blackbeard (Edward Teach)
François L'Olonnais

Long Ben (Henry Every)
Sir Francis Drake
**Sir Henry Morgan**
William Kidd

**Library of Congress Cataloging-in-Publication Data**
Nardo, Don, 1947-
 Sir Henry Morgan / Don Nardo.
     pages cm. — (Pirates around the world : terror on the high seas)
 Summary: "England's Sir Henry Morgan was one of the most feared pirates in history. However, he hated it when people called him that. He felt he was a patriot. True, he sank many ships, fought bloody battles, and stole gold from the Spanish. But these feats, he claimed, were done for, and with the support, of his beloved King"—Provided by publisher.
 Audience: Ages 8 to 11.
 Includes bibliographical references and index.
 ISBN 978-1-68020-077-5 (library bound)
 1. Morgan, Henry, 1635?-1688—Juvenile literature. 2. Pirates—Caribbean Area—Biography—Juvenile literature. 3. Pirates—England—Biography—Juvenile literature. 4. Buccaneers—Biography—Juvenile literature. 5. Caribbean Area—History—To 1810—Juvenile literature. 6. Spanish Main—History—Juvenile literature. I. Title.
 F2161.M83N37 2016
 972.9'03092—dc23
 [B]
                                                                    2015018395

eBook ISBN: 978-1-68020-078-2

# Contents

**INTRODUCTION: Struck by Sudden Disaster** ...........................................4

**CHAPTER 1**
  **Rise to Fame and Fortune** .............................................. 9
  **FROM SERVANT TO SURGEON** ...........................................13

**CHAPTER 2**
  **Dawn Assault on Portobello** ........................................15
  **CHANGING FLAGS**............................................................ 19

**CHAPTER 3**
  **Henry Morgan's Raid on Maracaibo** ...................... 21
  **SHIPS OF THE SEA RAIDERS** ............................................ 25

**CHAPTER 4**
  **Daring Escape from Lake Maracaibo** ................... 27
  **DRESSED LIKE A GENTLEMAN** ...........................................31

**CHAPTER 5**
  **The Burning of Panama City** ................................. 33
  **CUSTOMS AND RULES ABOARD PIRATE SHIPS** ..................37

**CHAPTER 6**
  **Henry Morgan in Popular Culture**........................38

Chapter Notes.........................................................................42
Works Consulted ................................................................. 44
Further Reading ................................................................. 44
On the Internet ................................................................. 45
Glossary.................................................................................. 46
Index........................................................................................47

Words in **bold** throughout can be found in the Glossary.

# INTRODUCTION
## Struck by Sudden Disaster

The terrible disaster struck on January 2, 1669, in a quiet Caribbean port. None who witnessed it were prepared for so much bloodshed and death. After all, they were happily celebrating two joyous occasions. The first was the New Year. The other was a recent announcement by the Welsh sea captain Henry Morgan, who fought for England. The swashbuckling adventurer had told the hundreds of sailors under his command that they would soon attack Cartagena de Indias—a Spanish colonial city on the northern coast of what is now Colombia, in South America. They hoped to seize a fortune in gold, silver and treasure.

### Pirate or Privateer?
The Spaniards considered Morgan a pirate or a buccaneer. But Morgan dismissed that charge as a gross insult. Pirates and buccaneers were outcasts and lawbreakers who attacked shipping, raided towns, and robbed people of their money and sometimes their lives. In contrast, Morgan proudly called himself a **privateer**. This was a legal version of a pirate akin to being a freelance soldier. Privateers were individuals who had a **letter of marque and reprisal** from their government and king permitting them to attack enemy ports and shipping during wartime. In lieu of a salary, privateers were allowed to keep most of the enemy property they confiscated. True, England and Spain had not officially declared war at the time the **catastrophe** occurred.

But Morgan's spies had recently advised him that Spain was secretly preparing to attack Jamaica. That English island-colony was located some 90 miles (145 kilometers) south of the larger Spanish island of Cuba. Morgan was then second in command to Jamaica's governor, his friend Sir Thomas Modyford. The two made a fateful decision: they would prevent the Spanish assault on Jamaica by striking Cartagena first.

To that end, Modyford equipped Morgan with a formidable new **flagship**. Named *HMS Oxford* after the well-known English university town, the vessel sported at least thirty-four guns. (Some accounts claim it had thirty-six.) In naval terms, a **gun** was an iron cannon that could inflict considerable damage on an enemy ship or fort.

## Meeting at Cow Island

Late in 1668, Morgan issued a call for privateers and buccaneers to assemble for his expedition against Cartagena. Ten vessels, carrying more than eight hundred men, answered that call to arms and hope for riches. They had no inkling that an unexpected calamity would soon send many of them to watery graves in **Davy Jones' Locker**.

The ships joined the *Oxford* at Isla Vaca, Spanish for "Cow Island." About 6 miles (10 kilometers) across, that pleasant place was situated not far south of the much larger island of Hispaniola. (Today, Hispaniola is split between French-speaking Haiti and the Spanish-speaking Dominican Republic. Isla Vaca is now called Île-à-Vache.)

When the boats had all dropped anchor, Morgan invited their captains aboard the *Oxford*. First, he said, they would have a banquet to celebrate the New Year. In addition, they would "feast one another for joy of their new voyage." (These words were recorded by a writer who interviewed some of

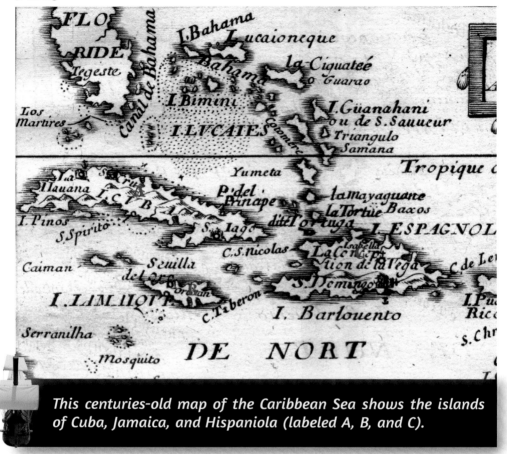

This centuries-old map of the Caribbean Sea shows the islands of Cuba, Jamaica, and Hispaniola (labeled A, B, and C).

the survivors.) During the lavish feast in Morgan's cabin, the ship captains raised countless toasts to one another's health. They also fired "many guns, the common sign of mirth among seamen."[1] The sounds of these cannons firing echoed through the harbor.

## Human Hands, Legs and Heads

Then disaster struck. Suddenly, the boom of the cannon was dwarfed by a deafening blast. A gigantic explosion tore through the *Oxford*, shattering her from **bow** to **stern**. Sailors on the decks of nearby vessels witnessed a blinding flash, and were pelted by a monstrous rain of debris. The gruesome mix included wood splinters, shrapnel, burnt flesh and human hands, legs and heads.

Some of the bloody body parts came from those dining at Morgan's table. Bizarrely the blast spared some diners while killing others. Those captains sitting facing Morgan were torn to shreds. But the expedition leader and those sitting beside him were blown through the cabin's windows and plunged into the harbor. As a result, though badly shaken, they survived.

The enormous explosion killed more than 250 privateers, most of them aboard the *Oxford*. That represented nearly a third of Morgan's force. Afterward, it became clear that some sailors who had survived the blast itself drowned because they were so drunk. As the writer put it, several sailors "might have escaped, had they not been so much overtaken with wine."[2]

The disaster was caused by the explosion of the flagship's gunpowder. But no one knows what ignited the blast. Perhaps a drunken sailor accidentally dropped his lit pipe, and a glowing spark made contact with one of the hundreds of kegs of the highly explosive powder. Hearing about the disaster, the Spaniards had a different explanation. They claimed a statue of Cartagena's Roman Catholic patron saint, Nuestra Señora de la Popa, miraculously came to life, flew to Isla Vaca, and blew up the *Oxford*.

Whatever caused the sinking of Morgan's flagship, the disaster did not deter the privateer from what he saw as his duty. After all, he was an English patriot, and Spain was England's mortal enemy. As such, Morgan fought many battles against the Spaniards. His colorful exploits became legendary, both in his own era and for all time. People saw him as the greatest privateer of them all in the storied era of Caribbean piracy!

A nearly 400-year-old drawing depicts Henry Morgan carrying the standard weapons of his era.

# Rise to Fame and Fortune

**N**o one knows exactly when or where Henry Morgan was born. As to *when*, the best guess of modern historians is sometime in 1635. Regarding *where*, it was someplace in Wales, which then as now was part of Great Britain. Morgan's hometown may have been Llanrhymny (today known as Llanrumney), on Wales' south coast. But other Welsh towns claim him as a native son as well.

Equally vague are details of Morgan's family and boyhood. In fact, not until he was close to thirty did he burst upon the historical stage. One account claims that when he was twenty or so, he was kidnapped and taken to England's Caribbean Sea colony of Barbados. There, according to one version of his early life, he worked as an indentured servant on a local plantation. Eventually he escaped the island and joined the English military. A different account claimed that he entered the army while still in England and was never kidnapped or enslaved.

## The English vs. the Spaniards

Whatever way Morgan became a soldier, he was living in Barbados in the mid-1650s. At the time, English leaders were preparing to attack the Spanish colony of Hispaniola. England and Spain, and their respective colonies in the New World, fought frequent wars in those days of imperial

expansion. The Spaniards had been the first Europeans to build up an overseas empire in the region. Beginning with Christopher Columbus, who first crossed the Atlantic Ocean in 1492, the Spanish created a string of colonies running from South America northward into Mexico, the Caribbean, Texas and Florida. Collectively, these outposts were called the Spanish Main.

England (as well Portugal, France, the Netherlands, Denmark and Sweden) established colonies in the New World decades after Spain. The various overseas empires quickly came into conflict with each other. Spain wanted the New World's territory and riches for itself. So its powerful fleets did not hesitate to attack foreign ships and settlements.

For their part, the English detested the Spaniards. They never forgot the Spanish Armada of 1588, an unsuccessful invasion of England by a huge Spanish fleet. Some of the leading English colonists in Jamaica explained why they loathed the Spaniards. Spanish raiders "continue all acts of hostility," they said. They were always "taking our ships and murdering our people." Moreover, the Spaniards regularly abused the Englishmen they took prisoner. The captives were "forced to work in the water from five in the morning till seven at night." And when the poor souls were starving and exhausted, they were "knocked down and beaten" with clubs and whips.[1]

## Becoming a Privateer

Cases like these contributed to young Henry Morgan's hatred of the Spaniards. A staunch English patriot, he eagerly fought with English forces against Spanish interests in the Americas. Morgan was among the close to seven thousand English fighters who invaded Hispaniola in 1655.

The attackers included Admiral William Penn, the father of William Penn, who founded Pennsylvania. Morgan and his comrades had high hopes for the venture. After all, their raiding force was huge for the time and place. But Morgan proved to be overconfident. Disease and tropical storms took an awful toll on his forces. After more than two thousand men died, they cut their losses and departed.

The expedition leaders wanted to save face in the eyes of their superiors in England. So they sailed with their remaining force to attack Jamaica. Then a Spanish possession, the island was nearly defenseless. This time Morgan and his fellow invaders were successful. For more than three centuries thereafter, Jamaica remained an English colony, until the island gained independence in 1962.

Morgan thrived in Jamaica. There he met and became good friends with the new colony's first governor, Sir Thomas Modyford. Soon Morgan became socially influential among the colonists. Longing to be more than a mere soldier, he decided to become a sea captain. To train himself in that profession, he joined a local company of privateers. According to the account of one of his later followers, Alexandre (or John) Esquemeling (ES-kuh-melin), "he soon learned their manner of living."[2]

The privateers' next few voyages proved highly profitable. With his share of the loot, Morgan bought a small ship. It proved an **opportune** time to do so. The English decided to use privateers to protect and enrich Jamaica. This was cheaper than stationing regular troops on the island.

To that end, in 1663 Governor Modyford called on Morgan to attack Spain's largest colony. Consisting of what is now Mexico, it was then called Nueva España meaning New Spain. Along with four other English privateers, Morgan returned from the plundering of Campeche,

Mexico, with a fortune in Spanish treasure. He followed up with other successful raids. Soon the Spaniards came to fear him as the seafaring terror of the Americas.

## Somewhere in Between?

The word *terror* was no exaggeration when applied to Henry Morgan. The privateer earned a reputation for brutality. Modern historians question whether this was more fiction than fact. First, much of what is known about Morgan's exploits comes from Esquemeling's account *De Americaensche Zee-Roovers* (Buccaneers of America) published in Amsterdam, Holland, in 1678. Esquemeling tended to exaggerate. Perhaps hoping to sell more books, he may have depicted Morgan as more bloodthirsty than he actually was.

Possible proof for this appears in Philip Ayres' *The Voyages and Adventures of Captain Barth, Sharp and Others in the South Sea* published in 1684, six years after Esquemeling's account. Ayres said that "all those cruelties" credited to Morgan were "contrary" to his nature. Indeed, he wrote, no man "behaved himself with more true valor" than Morgan.[3]

But some scholars think that Ayres too may have been exaggerating. Perhaps, they say, Morgan paid Ayres to write flattering things about him. Even Esquemeling occasionally portrayed Morgan in a positive light. In one case, he noted, one of Morgan's Englishmen stabbed a French sailor in the back. Morgan could easily have allowed his fellow countryman to escape punishment. Instead, he put "the criminal in chains" and ordered the attacker "to be carried to Jamaica, promising he would see justice done."[4]

Thus, it appears that Morgan was not all bad, as some people of his day claimed. Yet it is likely that he was not all good either. As is the case with most colorful historical characters, the truth is probably somewhere in between.

## From Servant to Surgeon

The chief source of information about Henry Morgan is the book *Buccaneers of America* published in Dutch in 1678. The author was John Esquemeling, whose first name is sometimes listed as Alexander, or Alexandre in French. Some accounts call him a Frenchman. Others say he was Dutch or Flemish. The confusion stems from the fact that he was born in France (in about 1645) but spent most of his life in Holland, and wrote in Dutch.

As a young man, Esquemeling traveled to the Caribbean island of Tortuga. There, he worked as a slave-like servant for a well-to-do colonist. At some point, likely in 1666, his master sold him to a mean-spirited individual, who abused him. When this caused Esquemeling to become seriously ill, the second master sold him to a third owner. Fortunately for the young man, his newest slave master was a kind-hearted surgeon who treated Esquemeling well, and even taught him his trade. Thus, it was in the capacity of a ship's doctor that Esquemeling joined Morgan's band of privateers in the late 1660s.

*Page 1 of* Buccaneers of America

In 1668, Morgan and his men attack Puerto de Principe, in what is now Cuba.

# Dawn Assault on Portobello

**B**eginning with his successful raid on New Spain in 1663, Morgan continued to pose a threat to the Spanish Main. In **retaliation**, the Spaniards plotted revenge. Early in 1668, Governor Modyford heard rumors that the Spanish might attack Jamaica soon. Summoning Morgan, by now his right-hand man, Modyford ordered him to attack Puerto Principe, then Cuba's second-richest city after the capital Havana. The goal was to collect information about the coming Spanish assault on Jamaica. A secondary aim was to gather gold and other loot.

The expedition set out in March 1668 and produced mixed results. Morgan did capture Puerto Principe, and he discovered some valuable information about Spanish military strength in the region. But the treasure he collected was far less than he had hoped for. He soon decided not to waste any more time in Cuba. Puerto Principe's leading citizens feared the dreaded privateer would destroy their town before departing. As Morgan wrote in the mission's official report, they begged him not to "fire the town or bring away prisoners." Their pleas were heard. Morgan took pity on them and "released them all."[1]

## More Challenging and More Dangerous

By the time Morgan left Cuba, it was mid-summer 1668. His men were disappointed that their venture had generated so little in treasure. As Esquemeling put it, the haul of **booty** was "not sufficient to pay their debts at Jamaica." So "Captain Morgan proposed they should think on some other enterprise" to fill their pockets.[2]

The "enterprise" Morgan chose was bigger than any he had ever attempted. He decided to loot Portobello, a key Spanish colonial port located on the Caribbean coast of the Isthmus of Panama. Portobello was then one of the richest places in the entire Spanish Main. The town, meaning "beautiful port," was a vital transfer point for the gold and silver the Spanish mined in Peru, in northwestern South America. The treasure chests were hauled overland to Portobello. And from there, heavily armed ships, called galleons, transported the wealth to the port of Cadiz in Spain.

Not surprisingly, with so much treasure passing through Portobello, the port was heavily defended. Three stone castles guarded it. One featured twelve cannon and a hundred soldiers. The second was armed with even more firepower—thirty-two cannon and two hundred men.

However, the third castle was still under construction and had fewer than ten soldiers. Morgan's spies had advised

*Model of a seventeenth-century Spanish galleon.*

him about this weak point, and he planned to exploit it. He also knew that besides the castles, cannon and soldiers, there were few obstacles to overcome. In Esquemeling's words, the town was "inhabited by only about four hundred families."[3]

## "Great Quantities of Stones"

Morgan launched his assault on Portobello shortly before dawn on July 10, 1668. Astutely, he had earlier anchored his ships well down the coast, several miles from the city. Then his fighters—more than five hundred strong—employed canoes to sneak up on their target. Reaching the beaches near Portobello at sunrise, they ditched their landing craft and rapidly moved on the city. The attack was so sudden that the defenders in the first castle managed to fire only a single cannonball. It flew harmlessly over the English attackers' heads!

As the invaders raced toward the town, the inhabitants fell into a panic. Because many of them were well-to-do, they were worried about their valuables. According to Esquemeling, who was among the attackers, they "cast their precious jewels and money into wells." Or they "hid them in places underground." That way, they might not be "totally robbed."[4]

After Morgan had captured the town and first castle, he turned his attention to the other two forts. The soldiers in those **garrisons** fought bravely. "The Spaniards let fall great quantities of stones from the walls," Esquemeling wrote. They also threw down "earthen pots full of gunpowder."[5]

Esquemeling also claimed that Morgan used local priests and nuns as **human shields**. According to this account, the Englishmen approached the final castle hiding behind Spanish clergymen and sisters. It was hoped that the fortress defenders would hold their fire for fear of killing the innocent.

Esquemeling wrote: "The religious men and women" begged Morgan to spare their lives. But he refused to listen to their pleas. "Thus, many of the religious men and nuns were killed."[6]

## An Enormous Haul

Morgan's assault ended before noon. Along with the town, his raiders had captured all three castles. He quickly ran up the English flag and ordered his men to search high and low for gold, silver, jewels, and other riches.

In the end, the haul was enormous. The collection of silver bars and plate, gold and silver coins was worth roughly 100,000 **pesos**. That was the equivalent of many millions of dollars today.[7]

Having conducted one of history's biggest treasure raids, Morgan freed his prisoners and departed. The venture proved a triumph not only for him, but also for Jamaica. It also sent huge political waves through the Americas and Europe. For their part, the Spaniards were outraged. Spain and England were not officially at war at the time. Spain's angry king Carlos II now gave his own privateers the green light to raid Jamaica. In turn, that further escalated tensions between the two empires.

In the meantime, Morgan invested some of his money in land in Jamaica. Part of him hoped to settle down and enjoy a quiet life. But soon, partly because of his daring raid on Portobello, other adventures beckoned. The other part of him was still a bold man who found it all but impossible to turn down such golden opportunities.

## Changing Flags

The English flag that Morgan ran up on Portobello originated in 1606. Three years before, King James I had united the crowns, or ruling powers, of England, Scotland and Ireland (although at the time they remained separate countries from a territorial standpoint). That flag is not the one in use today, called the Union Jack. Rather, it dates to 1801. The year before, England, Scotland, and Ireland had come together to form a single nation-state—the United Kingdom of Great Britain and Ireland, usually referred to simply as the United Kingdom for short.

### War Crime or Tall Tale?

The attack on Portobello raised serious questions about Morgan's honor. The rumor quickly spread that he had used nuns and priests as human shields. And later, thanks to Esquemeling's account, this unsavory tale permanently remained part of Morgan's popular image. But did Morgan actually commit that war crime? Historians have long pored through the diaries and documents of the era. No solid evidence has been found supporting Esquemeling's claim about using priests and nuns as human shields. Morgan himself loudly denied the accusation. In fact, he was so deeply insulted by Esquemeling's account of the incident that he sued that writer's publisher. In turn, the publisher issued a **retraction**, saying he no longer accepted Esquemeling's account as truthful.

1606                                    1801

*This image comes from a seventeenth-century woodcut depicting the infamous privateer Henry Morgan.*

# Henry Morgan's Raid on Maracaibo

**M**organ's sacking of Portobello in 1668 was a huge success. It greatly increased his reputation as a capable privateer of the Spanish Main. It was no surprise, therefore, that many sailors from all across the Americas flocked to him. The common wisdom was that if they joined him in his future ventures, they too might strike it rich.

Sure enough, when Morgan put out a call later that year for privateers and buccaneers to join him, hundreds enlisted. This time the target was Cartagena, in what would later become Colombia. At least that was Morgan's initial plan. As his forces assembled at Isla Vaca, he disastrously lost his flagship and nearly his life. The explosion tore the *Oxford* to pieces and killed many sailors. Yet Morgan continued planning his next raid.

## In the Nick of Time

Having lost so many of his sailors, Morgan changed his target for one less heavily defended. Instead of Cartagena, he decided to attack Maracaibo, a Spanish colonial town that today is part of the South American country of Venezuela. Maracaibo is located on the western shore of the strait that connects brackish Lake Maracaibo with the Gulf of Venezuela and the Caribbean Sea. Morgan planned to sack

the town and plunder its citizens' valuables. Then, he would sail into the lake and attack the colonial town of Gibraltar.

The expedition reached the South American coast in early March 1669. Morgan concentrated first on capturing La Barra, the imposing Spanish citadel that protected the entrance to Lake Maracaibo. He was concerned that the stronghold's cannon would damage his fleet as it sailed into the lake.

This worry proved groundless. As Morgan's forces "drew nigh the fort," Esquemeling wrote, they "found nobody in it." The Spaniards had "deserted it not long before." They left behind a fuse attached to a barrel of gunpowder. The booby trap was designed to "blow up the pirates" after they had entered the fort.[1] Luckily for the Englishmen, they found and defused this bomb in the nick of time.

## Combing the Jungle

The privateers did not know that the soldiers manning the fort had hurried off to Maracaibo to warn the residents that Morgan was about to attack. Terrorized, the people picked up whatever goods they could carry and fled into the jungle.

Thus, Esquemeling explained, Morgan and his men found the town as deserted as the fort had been. They "searched every corner, to see if they could find any people that were hid."[2] But none could be found. So they spread out into the jungle looking to capture some colonists. Finding a few over the next few days, the raiders demanded that they hand over their valuables.

As it turned out, Morgan and his privateers found very little loot. So they decided to sail on to Gibraltar. With any luck, they assured one another, the haul would be better there.

But when the Englishmen reached the lakeside town, they discovered a similar scene. The inhabitants of Gibraltar had fled just at the people of Maracaibo had. Once again, Morgan's men spent days combing the forests. The few Spaniards they captured claimed they possessed no riches. The raiders tortured some of their captives to loosen their tongues. But little of value surfaced.

As a result, Morgan switched to a different tactic. According to Esquemeling, he freed the captives and ordered them to seek out the other townspeople. They must gather a sizable **ransom**, Morgan said. Or Gibraltar was doomed, for he would "burn it down to the ground!"[3]

Morgan's threat was never carried out. The Spaniards raised the ransom, said to be five thousand **pieces of eight**. While not the fortune Morgan had hoped for, it was enough for a small payday for him and his fighters. Also, by this time Morgan had heard that a Spanish fleet was en route to

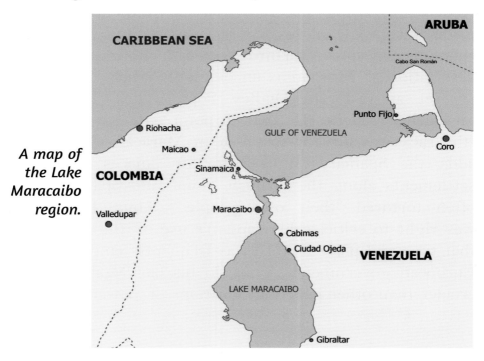

*A map of the Lake Maracaibo region.*

attack him. So he "made as much haste as he could for his departure," in Esquemeling's words.[4]

## Was Use of the Rack Unusual?

Modern historians are satisfied that most of the account of Morgan's Maracaibo raid is factual. But they are not so sure about one detail. Esquemeling wrote that after Morgan captured some of the local citizens, he tortured them. "All these miserable people" Esquemeling noted, "were put to the rack." This was "to make them confess where the rest of the inhabitants were, and their goods."[5]

The **rack** was a wooden torture device. The victim was laid flat on it and the operator tied ropes to the person's hands and feet. Pulling the ropes in opposite directions badly stretched the victim's body, dislocating limbs and inflicting horrible pain.

It has been documented that Morgan occasionally resorted to using the rack. But Esquemeling's account made it appear that his use of torture was routine. The claim of widespread torture seemed to confirm the writer's description of Morgan as uncommonly cruel.

Yet as historian Dudley Pope writes, Esquemeling misled his readers. "He fails to point out," says Pope, that "the rack was already installed in Maracaibo." Indeed, he adds, the Spaniards utilized torture devices in all their settlements along the Spanish Main. And Spanish leaders often tortured "their own people."[6] Thus, Esquemeling was right to criticize his captain's use of the rack. Yet in that time and place torture was frequently employed by all European governments. Thus, in his day Morgan was no crueler than other people in positions of power.

## Ships of the Sea Raiders

The privateers and pirates of Morgan's era employed a range of vessels to ply their trade. The earliest and smallest were fishing boats. These carried five to ten men and were powered by either oars or a single small sail.

Over time, however, raiders started employing bigger boats. The most common was the **pinnace** (PIN-is). Pinnaces ranged in length from about 15 to 50 feet (4.5 to 15 meters). The largest carried sixty men and had two or three moderate-sized sails. Such vessels were ideal for raiding because of their light weight. This allowed them to maneuver easily and escape from larger ships sent to capture or sink them.

On occasion, successful privateers managed to acquire a **frigate**, like Henry Morgan's ill-fated *Oxford*. This was a full-size warship equipped with numerous large sails and multiple cannon decks.

*Painting of a frigate*

Morgan barks orders at his soldiers during their daring escape from Maracaibo.

# Daring Escape from Lake Maracaibo

**D**uring the weeks in which Morgan raided Maracaibo and Gibraltar, Spanish officials did not sit idle. When news about the English attack got out, the leading Spanish admiral in the region was furious. His name was Don Alonzo de Campos y Espinosa. While he had only three warships at his disposal—the *Magdalena, San Luis*, and *Nuestra Señora*—they were well equipped with cannon. Thus although Morgan's fleet outnumbered his own, Don Alonzo felt confident of victory.

## "To Get Revenge"

The Spanish commander hoped to reach the narrow entrance to Lake Maracaibo before Morgan and his raiders escaped northward into the open sea. Luck seemed to be with Don Alonzo. Early in April 1669 he arrived at the entrance to the lake to find that his adversary was indeed still present. Don Alonzo placed his ships astride the narrow channel leading from the lake to the sea, thus trapping Morgan and his fleet.

Feeling he had the upper hand, the Spanish admiral sent a message to Morgan demanding that he return everything he had looted. "If you be contented to surrender," Don Alonzo said, "I will let you freely pass."[1]

But if Morgan resisted, the message stated, "I assure you" that "I will put your every man to the sword." The Spanish ships carried "very good soldiers," Don Alonzo warned. And they "desire nothing more ardently than to get revenge on you and your people."[2]

## Attack of the Fire Ship

Morgan informed his men of the Spanish admiral's **ultimatum**. Should they surrender, as Don Alonzo demanded? Or should they fight? The privateers chose the latter course, mainly because they did not want to give up their treasure. Morgan defiantly replied to Don Alonzo that the Spaniards should surrender. If they did not, he would make them regret it.

Don Alonzo scoffed at Morgan's boldness. The man must have a death-wish, the Spaniard reasoned. But he underestimated Morgan's brilliance as a tactician.

Morgan quickly thought of a plan to clear the Spanish vessels blocking the narrow channel. He would employ a naval trick called the "fire ship." One of his sailors had once seen it used. And he told Morgan: "We will fill her decks with logs of wood," standing upright "with hats." At a distance, these would look like men standing on the deck. "The same we will do at the port-holes,"[3] and they would create fake cannon as well. That way, the enemy would think a ship full of sailors was attacking.

In reality, however, the vessel would be loaded with kegs of gunpowder. A handful of hidden sailors would light the fuses and then escape in a rowboat. Meanwhile, the explosive-laden vessel would drift toward Don Alonzo's flagship, the *Magdalena*.

Sure enough, Morgan's scheme worked exactly as planned. On April 27, 1669, he launched the fire ship in the direction of the *Magdalena*. As the two vessels neared each other, the explosives aboard the English ship were ignited. Caught in the inferno, the Spanish frigate sank. While this was happening, several of Morgan's other ships bore down on the *Nuestra Señora*. In short order, his sailors boarded it and captured its crew.

The captain of the *San Luis* witnessed the naval battle. Wanting neither to be burned nor to be captured, he purposely grounded his ship, allowing his crew to escape ashore. As for Don Alonzo, he too managed to reach safety on dry land.

## Legendary Lore or Reliable History?

With the channel open, Morgan escaped and sailed back to Jamaica, arriving there on May 27, 1669. It was with enormous pride that he stood on the deck of his new flagship, formerly the Spanish frigate *Nuestra Señora*. Morgan received a hero's welcome. In addition to amassing much Spanish loot, he had cemented his reputation as the Caribbean's greatest privateer.

While Morgan became a legend in his own time, that fame sometimes made it hard for later generations to know exactly what he did. Controversy still surrounds the surviving accounts of many of his exploits.

His escape from Lake Maracaibo appears to be an exception, however. Historians have determined they have an accurate record of the naval battle. If Esquemeling's account had been the only one that survived, it might be different. After all, it has been shown that he often portrayed Morgan as more savage than he actually was.

But several other accounts of Morgan's escape from Lake Maracaibo have survived. One was written by the privateer William Dampier who later became the first

*A painted portrait of William Dampier, who wrote an account of Morgan's escape from Lake Maracaibo.*

Englishman to explore parts of what is today Australia. Another description of the battle was recorded by William Beeston, a well-to-do member of Jamaica's colonial elite. Still a third witness was Richard Browne who served for a time as Morgan's onboard surgeon. For the most part, all three descriptions of the battle jibe with Esquemeling's. As a result, Morgan's clever escape from Lake Maracaibo is more than just legend. It is reliable history.

## Dressed Like a Gentleman

**M**any people have difficulty visualizing what seventeenth century privateers and sea captains looked like. All too often, it is assumed that they dressed like Johnny Depp in the *Pirates of the Caribbean* films. The reality was different. In Hollywood movies, pirates are often dressed in filthy, stained clothes. But Captain Morgan regarded himself as a gentleman, and dressed like one. In keeping with the fashion of his day, he wore a clean white cotton shirt with wide sleeves and a scarf tied neatly around his neck. Over his shirt, he donned a dark-colored dinner jacket, also spotlessly clean, that hung well below his waist. He also wore breeches—pants that flared into a baggy mass around the thighs and gave way to tights from the knee down. His leather boots came half way up to the knees and had metal buckles. Sometimes he wore a triangular canvas hat. But on other occasions he went bareheaded, allowing his shoulder-length curly brown locks to hang loose.

A seventeenth-century engraving portrays Sir Henry Morgan and his chief officers conferring while behind them Panama City burns.

# The Burning of Panama City

After his triumph in Lake Maracaibo in 1669, Morgan could have rested on his laurels as an English national hero. But he was not yet ready to retire. He believed his king and country needed him. As a patriot, he could not allow Spain to threaten England's New World colonies.

Therefore, Morgan soon set his sights on the biggest Spanish prize yet. Panama City was one of Spain's largest and richest colonial outposts. It was located on the Pacific Ocean side of the Isthmus of Panama, on the opposite coast from Portobello, which Morgan had raided in 1668.

In those days, there was no Panama Canal linking the Atlantic/Caribbean coast to the Pacific side. (The Panama Canal was inaugurated in 1914.) Anyone wanting to reach Panama City had two choices. He could land on the Atlantic/Caribbean side and travel overland to the Pacific coast, or he could sail all the way around Tierra del Fuego at the tip of South America. The second option took several months and was fraught with danger.

## A Barn Full of Corn

Morgan opted for the overland route. He gathered an impressive force of more than eighteen hundred men. Boarding thirty-six ships, they departed Morgan's stronghold at Isla Vaca. Sailing without incident, they reached Panama

33

in December 1670. The trek across the isthmus began on January 9 of the following year.

Although not far as the crow flies, the trip took the men through dense tropical jungles. The steamy temperature reached 90° Fahrenheit (35° Celsius) or more every day. The humidity, heat and insects exhausted Morgan's men. Moreover, they expected to find provisions along the way so they left the Caribbean coast with little food. But Morgan's raiders found little to eat in the jungle wilderness.

The hungry sailors eventually happened on a farmer's barn filled with ears of corn. In Esquemeling's words, the privateers "beat down the doors." They then "ate it dry, as much as they could devour. Then they distributed a great quantity, giving every man a good allowance."[1]

## Battle on the Plain

Soon Morgan and his men were hungry again. On the ninth day of trudging through the jungle, a scout spotted Panama City. At the same time, they found a little valley filled with

*Parts of Panama City as they likely appeared in Morgan's time.*

farms. They gorged on the livestock. Some "killed and skinned cows, horses, and donkeys," Esquemeling wrote. Others "kindled fires and got wood to roast them." After cooking the animals, the **famished** men "devoured them with incredible haste." They gave no thought to the blood," which ran down from their beards to their waists."[2]

When his men had slaked their appetite and were ready to fight, Morgan pointed out their advantage. Since the Spanish defenders expected an attack to come from the sea, their cannon pointed out across the Pacific. Lacking the time to reposition their guns, that meant the Spanish would have to fight the privateers in the plain stretching before the city.

Sure enough the Spanish soldiers exited the town gate and lined up for battle. For several minutes, the combatants on both sides eyed each other warily. Then, Esquemeling recorded, "the Spaniards began to shout and cry, 'God save the king!' And immediately their horses moved against the pirates."[3]

*Spanish horse and foot soldiers like these fought the English at Panama City.*

The grueling battle lasted two hours, as the fighters attacked one another with guns, swords, knives and fists. Finally, according to Esquemeling, most of the Spanish force "was ruined," and most of its soldiers perished. "The rest fled," realizing "that they could not possibly prevail."[4]

## Who Torched the Town?

With its defenders either dead or fleeing, Panama City was wide open. After a brief contest for control of the streets, Morgan declared victory. A fire then broke out and burned down large portions of the town. Despite the blaze, Morgan and his men were able to collect the spoils they were seeking. Loading up more than two hundred mules with silver, gold and other valuables, the raiders departed the smoldering ruins of Panama City for the northern coast. A **controversy** arose over who had torched the town. The Spaniards blamed Morgan, and Esquemeling backed up that claim. The famous privateer "caused fire privately to be set to several great buildings of the city," he recorded.[5]

Based on Esquemeling's version, numerous writers and readers in later generations assumed Morgan torched the city. Modern historians question that claim. They point out that it made no sense for the English to burn the town. As historian Alexander Winston puts it, the charge was "absurd." After all, "burning Panama would destroy the very plunder that Morgan came for."[6]

Furthermore, Esquemeling ignored a simple fact. The city's Spanish commander later admitted to his superiors in Spain that before fleeing, he ordered the town's gunpowder stores be blown up. Most modern historians think that blast caused the conflagration. Thus while Morgan sacked Panama City, it seems unlikely that he torched it.

## Customs and Rules aboard Pirate Ships

Life aboard pirate ships and privateers' vessels was governed by strict rules. A captain's word was law. Sailors on such boats were capable of becoming violent and dangerous. Hard and fast regulations were needed to keep them in line. Thus, some captains whipped sailors for even the most minor offense. Indeed, punishments for more serious offenses could be extremely harsh. It was not unusual for a rule-breaker to have his nose slit off, or to be abandoned on an uncharted island. Capital punishment, "walking the plank," was not unheard of.

However some pirate ships operated in a democratic fashion. Before a voyage, the crewmen elected their captain and decided how loot would be divided. The sailors also agreed on a list of rules and punishments. Such pirate democracies were the exception rather than the rule.

# Henry Morgan in Popular Culture

$\mathbf{R}$eaction to the looting and burning of Panama City depended on one's nationality. The Spaniards viewed Morgan as a cruel and dangerous criminal who had wantonly destroyed a thriving city and murdered hundreds of innocent settlers. In contrast, Englishmen hailed him as a hero of epic proportions who had bravely stood up to the power-hungry Spaniards. In 1674, England's King Charles II knighted Morgan in appreciation for the colorful sea captain's bravery.

## Defending His Public Image

Morgan himself was well aware of the contrasting perceptions of his character and exploits. As he grew older, he grew increasingly concerned about his legacy. On the positive side, his countrymen loved him. Upon his return to Jamaica from his knighting in London, Morgan received a second major honor: the colony's government awarded him the post of assistant governor.

On the negative side, however, Morgan could not shake his reputation as a blood-thirsty pirate. Indeed even some Englishmen saw him that way. True, they happily celebrated his military deeds. But that was because they saw him as *their* brutal pirate, who looked after *their* interests. Offended by this portrayal, Morgan insisted he was a

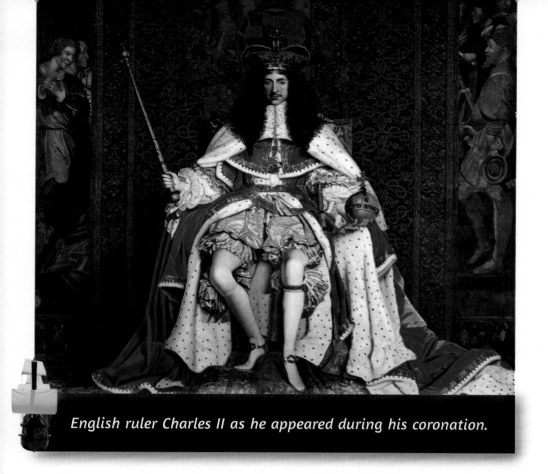

*English ruler Charles II as he appeared during his coronation.*

well-mannered gentleman whose raids had all been endorsed by English officials.

Much of this disagreement over Morgan's character stems from Esquemeling's book. Morgan's public image as a pirate *did* exist before the volume was published in 1678. However, from that time on this unsavory aspect of his reputation became much more pronounced.

Morgan's hope that suing the publishers would put an end to the blood-thirsty stories proved illusory. Even though the publishers printed a retraction, Esquemeling had the last laugh. His book became a bestseller across much of Europe and the Americas, and was translated into various languages. For centuries it remained the primary source about Morgan's exploits. While other historians wrote far

truer accounts, their books never enjoyed the popularity of Esquemeling's violence-filled narrative.

## Keeping the Historical Basis

After Sir Henry Morgan passed away in London on August 25, 1688, the negative public image of him that he detested prevailed. The majority of people in Jamaica and England remembered him as a pirate rather than a privateer. Yet Esquemeling's less than flattering biography ended up immortalizing Morgan. It established him as a renowned and colorful character for the ages.

Indeed, in the more than three centuries since Morgan died, his reputation has only grown. In all sorts of ways, millions of people still celebrate his exploits. And for that, he can mostly thank a man he came to despise—Esquemeling. Researcher Debbie Adams calls Esquemeling's exaggerated account a partly "imaginary collection that endured." Yet in spite of its failings, she adds, it gave rise to numerous "legends and myths of Hollywood and pulp fiction."[1]

By pulp fiction, Adams means accounts low in artistic quality but high in entertainment value. They have come to include poems, novels, movies and even video games. The most famous novel based on Morgan's life is Rafael Sabatini's 1922 bestseller *Captain Blood*. The real Morgan would no doubt have liked Sabatini. This is because the novelist pictured him as a decent, brave and likable person. (The hero, Peter Blood, is based partly on Morgan and partly on Henry Pitman, another historical figure of the same era.)

That romantic vision of a good man fighting for justice carried over into a number of so-called "pirate" films. One of the first was the 1935 movie *Captain Blood*. It starred another legend in his own time—the Hollywood **heartthrob**

Errol Flynn. The film owed its success in part to its realism. Like Sabatini, the filmmakers made the details of Morgan's era as accurate as possible. One of the screenwriters for *Captain Blood*, Casey Robinson, later recalled, "We kept the historical basis."[2]

## Confused yet Flattered

Hollywood churned out a series of movies featuring Henry Morgan or characters inspired by him. *The Black Swan* (1942) had a subplot about him during the time he was an English official in Jamaica. Morgan was also a character in *Blackbeard the Pirate* (1952), *Morgan the Pirate* (1961), and *Pirates of Tortuga* (also 1961).

Morgan's fame abounds in other areas of popular culture. The Celtic rock band Tempest enjoyed a hit song titled *Captain Morgan* in 1998. A decade later, in 2008, the Scottish heavy metal band Alestorm called their debut album *Captain Morgan's Revenge*.

Similarly, numerous resorts across the Caribbean and Central America have been named in his honor.

Adding to Morgan's fame is the brand of alcohol named for him. Canada's Seagram's distillery introduced its Captain Morgan's Rum in 1945. Thus, images of the swashbuckling privateer have become part of pop culture.

It is unclear what the real Henry Morgan would think of all this hype. Likely he would find it a bit confusing. Yet he would also be flattered that centuries after his death, people would still remember him with awe. After all, he saw himself as a servant of and heroic fighter for his king and country. Morgan would have been highly pleased by what a fellow Englishman said about him in 1738. He wrote, "He showed the world that he was qualified to govern as well as to fight." And "in all stations of life he was a great man."[3]

# Chapter Notes

**Introduction: Struck by Sudden Disaster**

1. John Esquemeling, *History of the Buccaneers of America*, translated by George A. Williams (New York: Frederick A. Stokes, 1914), pp. 135-136.

2. Ibid, p. 136.

**Chapter 1: Rise to Fame and Fortune**

1. British History Outline, *Calendar of State Papers, Colonial America and the West Indies*, vol. 5, October 5, 1668. http://www.british-history.ac.uk/report.aspx?compid=76528

2. Esquemeling, *History of the Buccaneers of America*, p. 101.

3. Quoted in Alexander Winston, *No Man Knows My Grave: Privateers and Pirates* (Boston: Houghton-Mifflin, 1969), p. 100.

4. Esquemeling, op cit, p. 121.

**Chapter 2: Dawn Assault on Portobello**

1. British History Outline, *Calendar of State Papers, Colonial America and the West Indies*, vol. 5, September 7, 1668. http://www.british-history.ac.uk/report.aspx?compid=76527

2. Esquemeling, *History of the Buccaneers of America*, p. 121.

3. Ibid, p. 125.

4. Ibid, p. 127.

5. Ibid, p. 127.

6. Ibid, p. 129.

7. It's impossible to know how much 100,000 pesos would be worth today. Too many centuries have gone by and too many factors have affected monetary values. Making things particularly sticky is that the word "peso" as used in books today in relation to old Spain is a bastardization of the term for a very old currency—the "peseta." This was not the same as a Mexican peso, which appeared much later. Moreover, both of those countries have repeatedly changed their currencies over the years.

# Chapter Notes

### Chapter 3: Morgan's Raid on Maracaibo
1. Esquemeling, *History of the Buccaneers of America,* p. 142.
2. Ibid, p. 143.
3. Ibid, p. 151.
4. Ibid, pp. 151–152.
5. Ibid, p. 143.
6. Dudley Pope. *The Buccaneer King: The Biography of the Notorious Sir Henry Morgan* (New York: Dodd and Mead, 1977), p. 173.

### Chapter 4: Daring Escape from the Lake
1. Esquemeling, *History of the Buccaneers of America,* p. 154.
2. Ibid, p. 154.
3. Ibid, p. 155.

### Chapter 5: The Burning of Panama City
1. Esquemeling, *History of the Buccaneers of America,* p. 199.
2. Ibid, pp. 205–206.
3. Ibid, p. 208.
4. Ibid, p. 209.
5. Ibid, p. 213.
6. Alexander Winston, *No Man Knows My Grave,* p. 79.

### Chapter 6: Morgan in Popular Culture
1. Debbie Adams, "The Molecularity of Being: Henry Morgan." http://lometa.blogspot.com/2009_05_24_archive.html
2. Quoted in Patrick McGilligan, editor. *Backstory: Interviews with the Screenwriters of Hollywood's Golden Age* (Berkeley: University of California Press, 1986), p. 299.
3. Quoted in E.A. Cruikshank, *The Life of Sir Henry Morgan* (New York: Macmillan, 1935), p. 419.

# Works Consulted

Black, Clinton. *History of Jamaica*. London: Churchill Livingstone, 1988.

Breverton, Terry. *Admiral Sir Henry Morgan: King of the Buccaneers*. New York: Pelican, 2005.

Cordingly, David. *Under the Black Flag: The Romance and Reality of Life Among the Pirates*. New York: Random House, 2006.

Cruikshank, E.A. *The Life of Sir Henry Morgan*. New York: Macmillan, 1935.

Esquemeling, John. *History of the Buccaneers of America*. Translated by George A. Williams. New York: Frederick A. Stokes, 1914.

Howard, Edward. *Sir Henry Morgan the Buccaneer*. Berkeley, CA: University of California Libraries, 2012.

Johnson, Charles. *A General History of the Robberies and Murders of the Most Notorious Pirates*. London: Routledge, 2013.

Latimer, Jon. *Buccaneers of the Caribbean: How Piracy Forged an Empire*. Cambridge, MA: Harvard University Press, 2009.

Pope, Dudley. *The Buccaneer King: The Biography of the Notorious Sir Henry Morgan*. New York: Dodd and Mead, 1977.

Pope, Dudley. *Harry Morgan's Way: A Biography of Sir Henry Morgan, 1635–1684*. London: Secker Warbury, 1977.

Steinbeck, John. *Cup of Gold: A Life of Sir Henry Morgan, Buccaneer*. New York: Penguin, 2008.

Tatty, Stephan. *Empire of Blue Water: Captain Morgan's Great Pirate Army*. New York: Three Rivers Press, 2008.

Winston, Alexander. *No Man Knows My Grave: Privateers and Pirates*. Boston: Houghton-Mifflin, 1969.

# Further Reading

Beahm, George. *Caribbean Pirates: A Treasure Chest of Fact, Fiction, and Folklore*. Newburyport, MA: Hampton Roads, 2007.

Charles River Editors. *Legendary Pirates: The Life and Legend of Captain Henry Morgan*. Charleston, SC: Create Space, 2013.

Konstam, Angus. *Pirate: The Golden Age*. London: Osprey, 2011.

Konstam, Angus. *World Atlas of Pirates*. Guilford, CT: Globe Pequot Press, 2009.

Kull, Kathleen and Kathryn Hewitt. *Lives of the Pirates*. Boston: Harcourt, 2010.

Laughton, John K. *Henry Morgan, Pirate: A Short Biography*. San Francisco: Shamrock Eden, 2011.

Platt, Richard. *Pirate!* London: Dorling Kindersley, 2007.

Stockton, Frank R. *Buccaneers and Pirates*. Mineola, NY: Dover Maritime, 2007.

# On the Internet

Adventures in History Land, "King's Pirate: Henry Morgan's Attack on Panama." (The first of three parts) http://adventuresinhistoryland.wordpress.com/2012/03/28/kings-pirate-henry-morgans-attack-on-panama-part-1/

Kennedy Hickman, "Privateers and Pirates: Admiral Sir Henry Morgan." http://militaryhistory.about.com/od/naval/p/morgan.htm

Hobby World, "Satisfaction: Privateer Galleon, 1668." http://www.hobbyworldinc.com/plast88.html

Museum of Unnatural History, "The Golden Age of Piracy." http://www.unmuseum.org/pirate.htm

Oceans Discovery, "Sir Henry Morgan." http://www.oceansdiscovery.com/pirates/sir-henry-morgan/

Samir S. Patel, "Pirates of the Original Panama Canal: Searching for the Remains of Captain Henry Morgan's Raid on Panama City." http://www.archaeology.org/issues/79-1303/features/543-pirates-henry-morgan-panama-city-raid

Wales Online, "Remains of Infamous Welsh Pirate Henry Morgan's Ship Finally Found After 340 Years." http://www.walesonline.co.uk/news/wales-news/remains-infamous-welsh-pirate-henry-1815546

# Glossary

**ardently** (AR-dint-lee)—eagerly

**booty** (BOO-tee)—treasure, valuables, or loot

**bow** (BOW)—the front part of a ship

**catastrophe** (k'TASS-truh-fee)—a terrible disaster

**controversy** (KON-troh-vers-ee)—a major or serious difference of opinion

**Davy Jones' Locker** (DAI-vee JONZ LOK-er)—a slang expression for death at the bottom of the ocean

**famished** (FAM-isht)—starving

**flagship** (FLAG-ship)—the lead vessel in a fleet of ships

**frigate** (FRIG-it)—in the age of sailing ships, a large warship, usually carrying many cannons

**garrison** (GAIR-i-sun)—a group of soldiers guarding or defending a military base or installation

**gun** (GUN)—when used as a naval term, a cannon

**heartthrob** (HART-throb)—a person, usually a celebrity, who is widely seen as a romantic or sexy character

**human shields** (HU-min SHEELDziln a military encounter, ordinary people that the soldiers on one side hide behind, hoping to escape death or injury. Using human shields is usually seen as cowardly and unethical

**letter of marque and reprisal** (LET-er uv MARK and ree-PRIZ-l)—a letter from a king or other ruler giving permission for a sea captin to attack an enemy

**opportune** (op-er-TUNE)—favorable or helpful

**peso** (PAY-soh)—in the seventeenth century, the main unit of Spanish currency. In those days, several thousand pesos was seen as a small fortune.

**pieces of eight** (pee-siz-uv-ATE)—in the seventeenth century, Spanish dollars

**pinnace** (PI-nis)—a small sailing ship—about the size of a large modern lifeboat—that was frequently used by early seventeenth-century pirates

**privateer** (prie-vuh-TEAR)—a person—usually a sea captain—who makes war on a an enemy at the request and with the support of his own government

**rack** (RAK)—a torture device that stretches a person's body in unnatural painful ways

**ransom** (RAN-sum)—money or valuables demanded by a person who has threatened to do something bad or destructive in exchange for not doing it

**retaliation** (ree-tal-ee-AY-shun)—payback or revenge

**retraction** (ree-TRAK-shun)—a statement made to take back or deny something said or printed earlier

**stern** (STURN)—the aft or back end of a ship

# Index

Adams, Debbie  40
Alestorm (rock group)  41
Amsterdam  12
Australia  30
Ayres, Philip  12
Barbados  9
Beeston, William  30
*Black Swan, The*  41
*Blackbeard the Pirate*  41
Blood, Peter  40
breeches  31
Browne, Richard  30
Cadiz  16
Campeche  11
*Captain Blood* (film)  40
*Captain Morgan* (song)  41
*Captain Morgan's Revenge* (album)  41
Captain Morgan's Rum  41
Carlos II, King  18
Cartagena de Indias  4, 5, 21
Charles II, King  38–39
Colombia  4, 21
Columbus, Christopher  10
Cuba  5, 15
Dampier, William  29–30
Davy Jones' Locker  5
*De Americaensche Zee-Roovers*
    (Buccaneers of America, book)
    12–13
Denmark  10
Depp, Johnny  31
Espinoza, Don Alanzo de Campos y
    27–28
Esquemeling, Alexandre (or John)
    11–13, 16–18, 22–24, 29–30, 34–36,
    39–40
fishing boats  25
Florida  10
Flynn, Errol  41
France  10
frigate  25
Gibraltar  22–23
Hispaniola  5, 9, 10
HMS *Oxford*  5, 21, 25
Ireland  19
Isla Vaca  5, 21, 33
Isthmus of Panama  16, 33
Jamaica  5, 10–12, 15, 18, 29, 30, 38,
    40–41

James I, King  19
La Barra  22
Lake Maracaibo  21, 29–30, 33
Llanrhymny  9
London  38, 40
*Magdelena* (ship)  27–29
Maracaibo  21–24, 26–27
Mexico (New Spain)  10–12, 15
Modyford, Sir Thomas  5, 11, 15
*Morgan the Pirate* (film)  41
Morgan, Sir Henry  4–8, 9–14, 15–20,
    21–26, 27–32, 33–36, 38–41
Netherlands (Holland)  10, 12–13
*Nuestra Señora* (ship)  27, 29
Nuestra, Señora de la Popa  6
Panama Canal  33
Panama City  32–36, 38
Penn, William  11
Pennsylvania  11
pieces of eight  23
pinnace  25
*Pirates of the Caribbean* (film)  31
*Pirates of Tortuga* (film)  41
Pitman, Henry  40
Pope, Dudely  24
Portobello  16–17, 19, 33
Portugal  10
Puerto del Principe  14–15
rack  24
Robinson, Casey  41
Sabatini, Rafael  40–41
*San Luis* (ship)  27, 29
Scotland  19
Spanish Armada  10
Spanish Main  10, 15–16, 21, 24
Sweden  10
Tempest (rock band)  41
Texas  10
Tierra del Fuego  33
Union Jack  19
United Kingdom  19
Venezuela  21
*Voyages and Adventures of Captain
    Barth, Sharp and Others in the South
    Sea* (book)  12
walking the plank  37
Winston, Alexander  36

# About the Author

Historian and award-winning writer Don Nardo has published more than four hundred and fifty books for teens and children, along with a number of volumes for college and general adult readers. Many of these volumes are about the peoples of the ancient world and their cultures. Others deal with colorful characters in medieval and early modern times, including explorers, soldiers, inventors and pirates. Mr. Nardo also composes and arranges orchestral music. He lives with his wife Christine in Massachusetts.